J

D0773678

Killer Whale

The World's Largest Dolphin

by Natalie Lunis

Consultant: Jenny Montague
Assistant Curator of Marine Mammals
New England Aquarium
Boston, MA

BEARPORT
PUBLISHING

New York, New York

Credits

Cover, © A & J Visage/Alamy; TOC, © Phase4Photography/Shutterstock; 4, Kathrin Ayer; 4–5, © Martin Ruegner/Imagestate/Photolibrary; 6, © George McCallum/SeaPics; 7, © CostinT/iStockphoto; 8L, © Brandon Cole Marine Photography/Alamy; 8R, © Rickman/Shutterstock; 9, © Gerard Lacz/Animals Animals Enterprises; 10, © Frank Greenaway/Dorling Kindersley/DK Images; 11, © Ingrid Visser/SeaPics; 12–13, © Francois Gohier/Ardea; 14, © Gerard Lacz/Animals Animals Enterprises; 15, © Gerard Lacz/Animals Animals Enterprises; 16T, © Johnny Johnson/Animals Animals Enterprises; 16B, © Flip Nicklin/Minden Pictures; 17, © D. Parer & E. Parer-Cook/Ardea; 18–19, © Brandon D. Cole/Brandon Cole Marine Photography; 20–21, © Juniors Bildarchiv/Photolibrary; 22L, © Masa Ushioda/SeaPics; 22C, © Doug Perrine/SeaPics; 22R, © Steve Noakes/Shutterstock; 23TL, © Ingrid Visser/SeaPics; 23TR, © Jan Daly/iStockphoto; 23BL, © Gerard Lacz/Animals Animals Enterprises; 23BR, © Evgeniya Lazareva/iStockphoto; 23BKG, © CostinT/iStockphoto.

Publisher: Kenn Goin
Editorial Director: Adam Siegel
Creative Director: Spencer Brinker
Original Design: Otto Carbajal
Photo Researcher: Picture Perfect Professionals, LLC

Library of Congress Cataloging-in-Publication Data

Lunis, Natalie.
  Killer whale : the world's largest dolphin / by Natalie Lunis.
    p. cm. — (More supersized!)
  Includes bibliographical references and index.
  ISBN-13: 978-1-936087-27-3 (library binding)
  ISBN-10: 1-936087-27-8 (library binding)
  1. Killer whale—Juvenile literature. I. Title.

QL737.C432L86 2010
599.53'6—dc22

                    2009027207

For more information, write to Bearport Publishing Company, Inc., 101 Fifth Avenue, Suite 6R, New York, New York 10003. Printed in the United States of America in North Mankato, Minnesota.

022011
021011CGC

10 9 8 7 6 5 4 3

Contents

A Whale of a Dolphin

The killer whale is the biggest dolphin in the world.

It can be up to 32 feet (10 m) long.

That's about as long as five tall adults lying end to end.

Many people think
that whales and dolphins are two
different kinds of animals, but they are
not. Every animal in the dolphin family—
including the killer whale—
is a kind of whale.

At Home in the Sea

Killer whales live in all the world's oceans.

They are most common in the freezing cold waters near the North and South Poles.

Killer whales have a thick layer of fat called blubber under their skin. The blubber helps them stay warm in cold ocean waters.

Killer Whales in the Wild

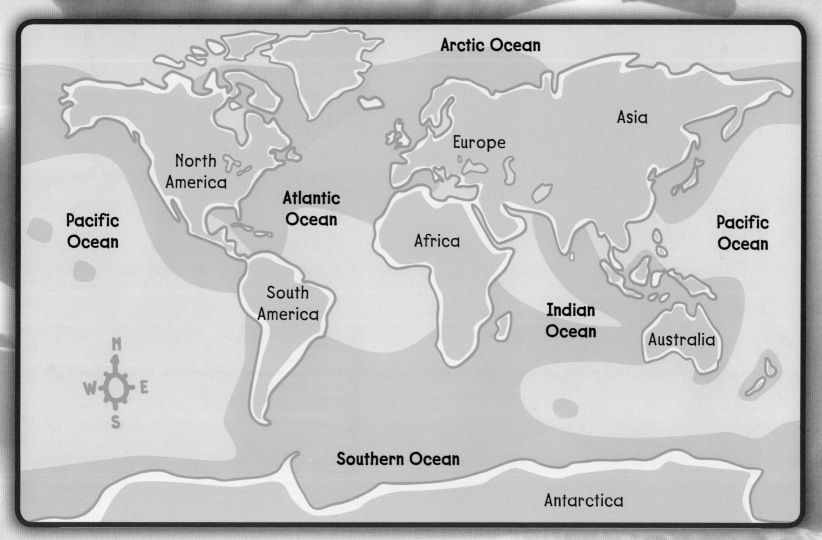

Arctic Ocean

Asia

Europe

North America

Atlantic Ocean

Pacific Ocean

Africa

Pacific Ocean

South America

Indian Ocean

Australia

N W E S

Southern Ocean

Antarctica

Where killer whales live

Strong Swimmers

Killer whales are powerful swimmers.

They move their strong tails up and down as they swim at speeds of up to 30 miles per hour (48 kph).

That's faster than any other kind of whale.

tail

Breathe In, Breathe Out

Unlike a fish, a killer whale cannot breathe underwater.

Instead, it needs to come up to breathe air.

It takes a deep breath through the **blowhole** on the top of its head.

Then it dives back down into the water.

A few minutes later, it comes back up, breathes out, and takes in another big breath.

blowhole

Family Life

Killer whales live in family groups called **pods**.

There are from 5 to 30 whales in a pod.

An older female whale leads the group.

She is the mother of some of the whales and the grandmother of others.

Female killer whales can live to be up to 75 years old. Males can live to be up to 60 years old.

Born to Be Big

A baby killer whale is called a **calf**.

When it is born, it is already much larger than an adult human.

It is 7 feet (2 m) long and weighs about 300 pounds (136 kg).

The calf keeps growing until it is about 20 years old.

When fully grown, a killer whale can weigh as much as two elephants—about 22,000 pounds (9,979 kg).

calf

A killer whale calf stays close to its mother at all times. The mother feeds it milk from her body. She also protects it from enemies that might try to attack and eat it.

a calf drinking its mother's milk

Sea Food

Killer whales are big eaters.

A large adult can eat 500 pounds (227 kg) of food each day.

Some eat salmon and other large fish.

Others eat seals, sea lions, penguins—and even other kinds of whales and dolphins.

penguins

A killer whale has cone-shaped teeth that are up to four inches (10 cm) long. The whale uses them to grab and tear food—not to chew it.

a killer whale attacking sea lions

Hunting Together

Killer whales get their food by hunting.

The whales in a pod work together as they hunt.

One pod might swim in a circle around a large group of fish in order to trap and eat them.

Another pod might surround a huge whale, such as a gray whale.

Then the killer whales take turns attacking the giant animal.

Some people call killer whales the "wolves of the sea." That's because a pod of killer whales works as a team to hunt food—just like a pack of wolves.

a killer whale attacking a gray whale

Killer or Orca?

Some people call the killer whale by another name—orca.

They use this name because the large dolphin doesn't kill for the sake of killing.

It kills to get food so that it can survive.

Whichever name it is called, it is still the largest of all dolphins—and one of the fastest and most powerful animals in the sea.

The name "killer whale" comes from sailors who traveled on ships hundreds of years ago and saw killer whales attacking other whales. The name "orca" comes from scientists who study whales and other animals.

More Big Dolphins

Killer whales live in the water, but they are not fish. Killer whales, like all dolphins, belong to a group of animals called mammals. Almost all mammals give birth to live young instead of laying eggs. The babies drink milk from their mothers. Mammals are also warm-blooded and have at least a little bit of hair or fur on their skin. Killer whales are born with a few hairs near their mouth, which soon fall out.

Here are three more big dolphins. Like all dolphins, each one is also a kind of whale.

Pilot Whale

This member of the dolphin family is the second-largest dolphin in the world. It can be up to 24 feet (7.3 m) long.

False Killer Whale

This member of the dolphin family can be almost 18 feet (5.5 m) long.

Bottlenose Dolphin

This is the animal most people picture when they think of dolphins. The bottlenose dolphin is usually around 10 feet (3 m) long.

Killer Whale:
32 feet (10 m) long

Pilot Whale:
24 feet (7.3 m) long

False Killer Whale:
18 feet (5.5 m) long

Bottlenose Dolphin:
10 feet (3 m) long

Glossary

blowhole (BLOH-hohl) the opening on the top of a killer whale's head that allows the whale to breathe in new air and let out old air

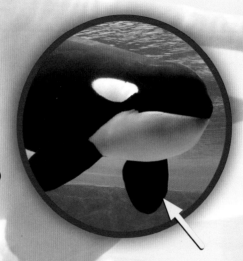

fin (FIN) a flap-like body part that a whale uses to steer while swimming

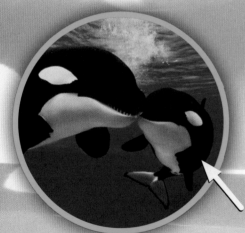

calf (KAF) a baby whale

pods (PODZ) family groups of whales

Index

Read More

Gentle, Victor, and Janet Perry. *Orcas: Killer Whales.* Milwaukee, WI: Gareth Stevens (2001).

Markle, Sandra. *Killer Whales.* Minneapolis, MN: Carolrhoda Books (2004).

Simon, Seymour. *Killer Whales.* New York: SeaStar Books (2002).

Learn More Online

To learn more about killer whales, visit
www.bearportpublishing.com/MoreSuperSized